Table of Contents:

Chapter Summaries:

1. Introduction: Embracing the Digital World

   - The shift from traditional brick-and-mortar stores to digital platforms
   - Benefits of operating an antique shop online
   - Overview of the book

2. Assessing Your Passion for Antiques

- Understanding your motivation for entering the antique business
- Analyzing your interests and strengths
- Cultivating a passion for antiques and history
3. Crafting Your Antique Shop Vision and Business Plan
    - Defining your target market and niche
    - Creating a business plan
    - Setting goals and milestones
4. Sourcing and Curating Antiques for Your Digital Shop
    - Where to find antiques: auctions, estate sales, flea markets, etc.
    - Authenticating and appraising antiques
    - Curating a collection that reflects your brand identity
5. Building Your Online Antique Store
    - Choosing the right platform for your store
    - Designing a user-friendly and visually appealing website
    - Search engine optimization (SEO) and site performance
6. Navigating Social Media and Online Marketing
    - Developing a social media strategy
    - Content creation, curation, and promotion
    - Utilizing analytics and insights to refine your marketing efforts
7. Developing Your Brand Identity and Online Presence
    - Crafting a compelling brand story
    - Creating a consistent visual identity
    - Building an engaged community around your brand
8. Customer Service and Engagement in the Digital Age
    - Providing excellent customer support
    - Encouraging customer reviews and feedback
    - Implementing a loyalty program
9. Expanding Your Network: Partnerships, Collaborations, and Events
    - Networking with other antique dealers and collectors

The Digital Antique Shop Owner:
A Modern Blueprint for a Timeless Business

Embark on a journey to transform your passion for antiques into a thriving digital business with this comprehensive guide to becoming a successful digital antique shop owner. This book will lead you through each step of the process, from building a solid foundation to expanding your digital empire.

Discover how to curate an exquisite collection, create a compelling online presence, and cultivate a loyal customer base in the ever-evolving world of e-commerce. Learn the art of forging connections, sharing expertise, and navigating challenges as you immerse yourself in the rich history and unique stories behind each antique piece.

As you delve into the world of digital antiques, uncover strategies for scaling your business, diversifying your offerings, and leveraging collaborations and partnerships to drive success. Embrace the opportunity to make a positive impact on the digital antique community by fostering unity, supporting fellow antique professionals, and contributing to the preservation of cultural heritage.

Packed with practical advice, insightful strategies, and inspiring stories, this guide is the ultimate blueprint for building a lasting, successful digital antique shop that stands the test of time. Whether you are a seasoned antique enthusiast or a newcomer to the world of antiques, this book will equip you with the knowledge, tools, and inspiration you need to create a thriving digital antique business and leave a legacy in the enchanting world of antiques and e-commerce.

Join us on this captivating adventure and unlock your full potential as a digital antique shop owner, igniting your passion for antiques and inspiring future generations to cherish the beauty and history of these timeless treasures.

Chapter 1: Introduction - Embracing the Digital World

Once upon a time, antique shops were synonymous with dusty, dimly lit spaces filled with curious objects from yesteryears, where the scent of old books mingled with the faint whiff of varnish. These brick-and-mortar stores were often tucked away in alleyways or nestled among quaint streets, beckoning passersby to step inside and travel back in time. While the allure of these treasure troves remains, a dramatic shift has occurred in the antique industry: the digital revolution.

The internet has transformed the way we live, work, and shop. This massive wave of digitalization has not spared the antique world, and shop owners, collectors, and enthusiasts alike have embraced the online realm. By opening a virtual door, antique shops now transcend geographic boundaries and offer their wares to customers around the globe.

In this first chapter, we will explore the transition from traditional brick-and-mortar antique shops to digital platforms, delve into the benefits of operating an antique shop online, and set the stage for the rest of the book.

The Digital Shift: A New Era for Antique Shops

The rise of e-commerce has democratized access to antiques, enabling enthusiasts to discover and purchase items from the comfort of their homes. Traditional antique shops, faced with the challenge of dwindling foot traffic, have adapted by expanding their online presence. Savvy shop owners have come to understand that the digital world offers unparalleled opportunities for growth and innovation.

While brick-and-mortar antique shops still have their charm, the digital landscape has removed many barriers that once hindered the expansion of these businesses. The global reach of the internet has enabled antique shop owners to display their collections to an international audience, increasing their chances of finding the perfect buyer for each unique piece.

Benefits of Operating an Antique Shop Online

The digital world offers numerous advantages for antique shop owners. Here are a few compelling reasons to consider launching your antique business in the digital realm:

- Lower overhead costs: Operating an online store eliminates the expenses associated with running a physical location, such as rent, utilities, and maintenance. This cost reduction allows you to focus your resources on sourcing and marketing exceptional antiques.
- Wider audience: An online antique shop is accessible to customers around the world, providing you with a much larger pool of potential buyers. This expanded reach can significantly boost your sales and revenue.
- Flexibility: Running an online business allows you to work from anywhere, at any time. You can manage your antique shop from the comfort of your home, or even while traveling in search of new treasures.
- Targeted marketing: The digital world offers sophisticated tools and platforms for reaching your ideal customers. With the help of analytics and targeted advertising, you can connect with individuals who share your passion for antiques and are likely to make a purchase.
- Enhanced customer experience: A well-designed online store enables customers to browse your collection at their own pace, view high-quality images, and access detailed information about each item. This level of convenience can result in higher customer satisfaction and repeat business.

With the rapidly evolving digital landscape, there has never been a better time to start an online antique shop. The following chapters of this book will serve as a comprehensive guide, providing you with the knowledge and tools needed to successfully launch and grow your digital antique business.

From discovering your passion for antiques to crafting your brand identity, we will explore every aspect of running a thriving online antique shop. Whether you are an experienced antique dealer looking to expand your business or a budding entrepreneur with a love for history, this book will help you navigate the exciting world of digital antiques and turn your dreams into reality.

So, without further ado, let us embark on this fascinating journey together and unlock the secrets of building a successful digital antique shop.

As we progress through the chapters, you will learn how to:

- Assess your passion for antiques and identify your unique strengths within the industry
- Develop a sharp vision and business plan that sets the foundation for your online antique store
- Source and curate a compelling collection of antiques that reflects your brand identity and appeals to your target market
- Build a visually appealing, user-friendly, and optimized website that drives traffic and converts visitors into customers
- Navigate social media and online marketing to reach your ideal audience and create a loyal community around your brand
- Deliver exceptional customer service in the digital age, fostering trust and long-term relationships with your clientele

- Leverage technology to streamline inventory management, logistics, and other operational aspects of your business
- Expand your network by forging partnerships and collaborations within the antique community, both online and offline
- Navigate the legal and ethical considerations associated with operating an online antique store
- Plan for long-term success by staying current with industry trends and continually adapting and growing your digital antique shop

With each chapter, we will delve into these topics in detail, providing you with practical insights and actionable advice to help you build a thriving online antique business. By the end of this book, you will be well-equipped to embrace the digital world and create a flourishing antique shop that is not only rooted in tradition and history but also poised to adapt and succeed in an ever-evolving landscape.

The digital revolution has ushered in a new era for the antique industry, and the opportunities for growth, innovation, and success are boundless. As you step into this exciting realm, remember that the core principles that have made antique shops enduringly popular – passion, authenticity, and a deep appreciation for the stories and history embedded in each unique piece – remain just as relevant in the digital world.

By embracing these timeless values while harnessing the power of modern technology and digital platforms, you will be well on your way to creating an antique shop that transcends the boundaries of the physical world and captures the hearts and minds of collectors and enthusiasts across the globe.

So, let us begin our journey into the world of digital antiques, where the past meets the present, and a treasure trove of opportunities awaits.

Chapter 2: Assessing Your Passion for Antiques

The antique business is a niche market that requires a deep-rooted passion for history, culture, and the objects that embody them. Before embarking on this journey, it is essential to understand your motivation for entering the antique world and assess your strengths, interests, and passions. This chapter will help you explore your connection to antiques and determine whether opening a digital antique shop aligns with your personal and professional aspirations.

Understanding Your Motivation

Antiques are more than just objects; they are tangible connections to the past, each with a unique story to tell. The allure of the antique business lies in discovering, preserving, and sharing these stories with others. For many, this passion is driven by a love for history, art, quality, or simply the thrill of the hunt.

To assess your motivation for entering the antique business, consider the following questions:

- What draws you to antiques? Are you fascinated by the history and stories behind these objects, or do you appreciate their artistic and aesthetic qualities?
- Have you always been drawn to collecting, or is it a newfound interest?
- Are you excited about the prospect of learning more about antiques and deepening your knowledge of various eras, styles, and cultural influences?
- Do you enjoy researching and authenticating items, and are you prepared to dedicate the necessary time and effort to acquire expertise in your chosen niche?

If you find yourself answering these questions positively, it is likely that your passion for antiques can fuel a successful digital antique shop.

As you contemplate opening a digital antique shop, take the time to analyze your interests and strengths, as these will play a crucial role in defining your niche and overall business strategy. Consider your areas of expertise, your favorite historical periods, and the styles or categories of antiques that resonate most with you.

Some questions to help you identify your interests and strengths include:

- What types of antiques are you most drawn to? Furniture, decorative objects, artwork, textiles, or something else entirely?
- Are there specific historical periods or styles that you find particularly appealing, such as Art Deco, Victorian, or Mid-Century Modern?
- Do you have any existing expertise in a particular area, either through education, work experience, or personal interests?
- What skills do you possess that could be valuable in running a digital antique shop, such as marketing, photography, restoration, or customer service?

Reflecting on these questions will help you identify the areas of the antique business that are most closely aligned with your interests and strengths. This self-awareness will be invaluable as you build a business that capitalizes on your passions and expertise.

Cultivating a Passion for Antiques and History

Whether you are a seasoned collector or a newcomer to the antique world, cultivating a passion for antiques and history is an ongoing process. To deepen your appreciation for the objects you will be dealing with and provide the best possible experience for your customers, you will need to continually expand your knowledge and understanding of the antique market.

Here are some suggestions for nurturing your passion and growing your expertise:

- Read extensively: Immerse yourself in books, magazines, and online resources that cover various aspects of antiques, including history, styles, and market trends. This will help you gain a comprehensive understanding of the field and stay informed about the latest developments.
- Visit museums and galleries: Exploring museums and galleries will deepen your appreciation for the quality, artistry, and historical context of antiques. Observing how these institutions curate and display their collections can also inspire your own approach to presenting antiques in your digital shop.
- Attend antique fairs and auctions: Regularly attending antique fairs, auctions, and estate sales will not only help you hone your eye for quality and value but also provide opportunities to network with fellow dealers, collectors, and enthusiasts. These events are excellent learning experiences and can offer insights into the current state of the antique market.
- Take courses and workshops: Enroll in courses or workshops that focus on specific areas of interest within the antique world, such as furniture restoration, ceramics, or silverware. This will help you develop specialized expertise that can set your digital antique shop apart from competitors.
- Join online communities and forums: Engage with fellow antique enthusiasts and professionals in online communities

and forums. These platforms offer invaluable opportunities to ask questions, share experiences, and learn from others who share your passion for antiques.

- Develop relationships with mentors and experts: Cultivate relationships with experienced antique dealers, appraisers, and collectors who can share their knowledge and insights with you. Their guidance can be invaluable in helping you navigate the complexities of the antique market and avoid common pitfalls.

By continually expanding your knowledge and appreciation for antiques, you will be better equipped to provide a unique and memorable experience for your customers. Your passion for history and the stories behind the items in your collection will also serve as a powerful marketing tool, enabling you to engage with your audience on a deeper level.

Conclusion

Before embarking on your journey as a digital antique shop owner, it is essential to ensure that your passion for antiques and history is genuine and enduring. As you delve deeper into the world of antiques, you will find that this passion is the driving force behind your business, propelling you through challenges and motivating you to continually learn and grow.

In the following chapters, we will help you translate this passion into a successful digital antique shop by guiding you through the process of crafting a compelling vision, developing a strategic business plan, and building an online presence that resonates with your target audience. Together, we will create a thriving digital antique business that not only celebrates the past but also embraces the opportunities of the digital age.

Chapter 3: Crafting Your Antique Shop Vision and Business Plan

With a passion for antiques firmly established, it is time to turn your dream of owning a digital antique shop into reality. The first step in this process is to create a sharp vision for your business and develop a strategic business plan that will guide your efforts as you build and grow your digital antique store. In this chapter, we will explore the importance of defining your target market and niche, as well as the key components of a comprehensive business plan.

Defining Your Target Market and Niche

A critical aspect of building a successful digital antique shop is identifying your target market and niche. Your target market refers to the specific group of customers you aim to serve, while your niche is the area of specialization within the antique market that sets your shop apart from competitors.

To define your target market and niche, consider the following questions:

- Who are your ideal customers? What are their demographics, interests, and preferences? Are they casual collectors, professional interior designers, or history enthusiasts?
- What types of antiques are you most passionate about and knowledgeable about? Are there specific styles, periods, or categories that you feel particularly drawn to?
- What unique value can you offer to your target customers that sets your digital antique shop apart from the competition? This could be your expertise in a specific area, a unique sourcing method, or exceptional customer service.

By answering these questions, you will gain a clearer understanding of the customers you want to attract and the distinctive niche that your digital antique shop will occupy.

A well-structured business plan serves as a roadmap for your digital antique shop, guiding you through each stage of building and growing your business. A comprehensive business plan should include the following key components:

- Executive Summary: A brief overview of your digital antique shop, including your vision, mission, and objectives.
- Business Description: A detailed explanation of your business concept, target market, niche, and unique selling proposition.
- Market Analysis: An assessment of the current state of the antique market, including trends, competitors, and potential opportunities and challenges.
- Marketing Strategy: A description of the methods you will use to reach your target customers, such as social media marketing, search engine optimization, and content creation.
- Operations Plan: An outline of the processes involved in sourcing, authenticating, and selling antiques, as well as managing inventory and shipping planning.
- Financial Projections: A forecast of your anticipated revenue, expenses, and profit margins over the next three to five years, along with a break-even analysis.
- Management and Organization: A description of the roles and responsibilities of key team members, as well as any potential partnerships or collaborations.

Setting Goals and Milestones

To ensure your digital antique shop remains on track for success, it is essential to set specific, measurable, achievable, relevant, and time-bound (SMART) goals and milestones. These goals should cover various aspects of your business, such as website traffic, sales revenue, social media engagement, and inventory turnover.

Regularly reviewing and adjusting your goals and milestones will help you stay focused on your priorities, measure your progress, and identify areas where adjustments may be needed.

Conclusion

Crafting a sharp vision and business plan is the foundation of your digital antique shop, providing you with the direction and guidance needed to navigate the challenges and opportunities that lie ahead. By defining your target market and niche and developing a comprehensive business plan that encompasses your marketing strategy, operations, and financial projections, you will be well-prepared to embark on the exciting journey of building a thriving digital antique business.

In the next chapter, we will delve into the world of sourcing and curating antiques for your digital shop, exploring the various methods and channels for finding unique and desirable items that will captivate your target audience and set your business apart from the competition.

We will discuss strategies for identifying valuable and authentic pieces, as well as the importance of building a curated collection that reflects your unique brand identity and resonates with your target customers. Additionally, we will examine the role of restoration and conservation in the antique business and provide guidance on how to preserve the integrity and value of the items in your collection.

Armed with a well-crafted vision, business plan, and a growing understanding of the antique market, you will be well on your way to creating a digital antique shop that not only captivates and inspires your customers but also stands the test of time in the ever-evolving digital landscape.

Chapter 4: Sourcing and Curating Your Antique Collection

A captivating and thoughtfully curated collection is at the heart of every successful digital antique shop. The items you choose to display will not only define your brand identity but also determine the overall appeal of your store to your target audience. In this chapter, we will explore the various methods and channels for sourcing unique antiques and curating a collection that resonates with your customers and sets your digital shop apart from the competition.

Sourcing Antiques: Methods and Channels

Finding high-quality and unique antiques requires a keen eye, patience, and persistence. There are numerous methods and channels through which you can source items for your digital antique shop. Some of these include:

- Estate Sales and Auctions: Attending estate sales and auctions can be an excellent way to find antiques at competitive prices. These events often feature a diverse range of items from various periods and styles, allowing you to discover hidden gems that can become the centerpiece of your collection.

- Flea Markets and Antique Fairs: Flea markets and antique fairs are treasure troves of one-of-a-kind items. Visiting these events regularly will help you build relationships with vendors, expand your network, and stay informed about the latest trends and market developments.
- Online Marketplaces and Auction Platforms: Online platforms such as eBay, 1stdibs, and Live Auctioneers offer a vast selection of antiques, often with detailed descriptions and photographs. While sourcing antiques online requires careful research and authentication, these platforms can provide access to rare and unique items from around the world.
- Antique Dealers and Wholesalers: Establishing relationships with reputable antique dealers and wholesalers can grant you access to exclusive items and competitive prices. Be sure to thoroughly vet potential suppliers to ensure the quality and authenticity of their merchandise.
- Private Sellers and Collectors: Networking with private sellers and collectors can lead to unique and high-quality antiques. Cultivating relationships within the antique community will help you discover pieces that may not be available through traditional channels.

Curating Your Collection

Once you have sourced a selection of antiques, the next step is to curate your collection in a way that reflects your unique brand identity and appeals to your target audience. Consider the following tips when curating your digital antique shop:

- Define Your Aesthetic: Your collection should embody a consistent aesthetic that reflects your niche and brand identity. Whether it is Art Deco, Victorian, or Mid-Century Modern, maintaining a cohesive style will help your digital shop stand out and attract your ideal customers.

- Balance Variety and Focus: While it is essential to offer a diverse range of items to cater to different tastes, avoid spreading yourself too thin. Focus on your strengths and expertise, and curate a collection that highlights your knowledge and passion for your chosen niche.
- Showcase Unique and Authentic Items: Stand out from the competition by featuring rare and authentic antiques that pique the curiosity and interest of your customers. Take the time to research, authenticate, and document the history and provenance of each item in your collection.
- Prioritize Quality Over Quantity: A smaller, high-quality collection is more appealing than a vast assortment of mediocre items. Focus on sourcing the best possible pieces for your digital shop, even if it means having a smaller inventory.
- Rotate Your Inventory: Regularly refreshing and rotating your inventory will keep your digital antique shop feeling fresh and dynamic. Introduce new items periodically to keep your customers engaged and encourage repeat visits.

Conclusion

Sourcing and curating a captivating collection of antiques is a critical aspect of building a successful digital antique shop. By leveraging various channels and methods for finding unique and desirable items, and carefully curating your collection to reflect your unique brand identity and niche, you will create a digital shopping experience that resonates with your target audience and sets your business apart from the competition.

In addition to sourcing and curating your collection, it's essential to continually refine and expand your knowledge of the antique market, stay abreast of trends and developments, and seek out opportunities for growth and collaboration within the antique community.

In the next chapter, we will delve into the world of digital storefronts and online marketing, exploring best practices for creating a visually appealing and user-friendly website, as well as strategies for leveraging social media, content marketing, and search engine optimization to drive traffic, increase visibility, and grow your digital antique business.

By combining a thoughtfully curated collection with a robust digital presence and effective marketing strategies, you will be well on your way to creating a thriving digital antique shop that captures the hearts and imaginations of antique enthusiasts around the world.

Chapter 5: Building Your Digital Storefront and Marketing Your Antique Shop

Creating an enticing and user-friendly digital storefront is crucial for displaying your curated collection of antiques and attracting customers to your online shop. In this chapter, we will discuss the essential elements of designing an effective website for your digital antique shop and explore marketing strategies that will help you reach your target audience, build brand awareness, and grow your business.

Designing Your Digital Storefront

Your website is the virtual representation of your antique shop, and its design should reflect your brand identity, aesthetic, and the overall shopping experience you want to create for your customers. Consider the following elements when designing your digital storefront:

- Choose a User-Friendly Platform: Select a website platform that is easy to navigate, customizable, and mobile-responsive. Popular e-commerce platforms such as Shopify, WooCommerce, and BigCommerce offer user-friendly templates and tools designed specifically for online shops.
- Showcase High-Quality Images: Invest in professional photography to capture the beauty and detail of your antiques. High-quality images are essential for conveying the value and authenticity of your items and enticing customers to make a purchase.
- Craft Engaging Product Descriptions: Write detailed and engaging product descriptions that highlight the history, provenance, and unique features of each antique. This information will not only help your customers make informed decisions but also highlight your expertise and passion for your niche.
- Implement Easy Navigation: Organize your inventory into clear categories and subcategories to help customers easily find and browse items that interest them. Use filters and sorting options to enhance the browsing experience further.
- Provide Secure and Convenient Payment Options: Offer a range of secure and reliable payment options to accommodate the preferences of your target audience. Integrate reputable payment gateways, such as PayPal and Stripe, to build trust with your customers.

Marketing Your Digital Antique Shop

To drive traffic to your digital storefront and increase visibility within your target market, you need to implement effective marketing strategies that leverage a variety of channels and platforms. Some key marketing tactics to consider include:

- Search Engine Optimization (SEO): Optimize your website with relevant keywords, well-structured content, and metadata to improve its visibility on search engines like Google. This will help potential customers find your digital antique shop when searching for items in your niche.

- Content Marketing: Create engaging and informative blog posts, articles, and videos that highlight your expertise and passion for antiques. Share your content on social media and in relevant online communities to attract potential customers and build credibility within your niche.

- Social Media Marketing: Establish a strong presence on platforms such as Instagram, Pinterest, and Facebook, where you can display your collection, share updates, and engage with your audience. Use eye-catching visuals, stories, and live streams to create an authentic connection with your customers.

- Email Marketing: Build an email list of subscribers and nurture relationships with your customers through regular newsletters, exclusive offers, and personalized content. This will help you maintain customer engagement and encourage repeat business.

- Collaborate with Influencers and Bloggers: Partner with influencers, bloggers, or other antique enthusiasts who share your target audience to increase your reach and credibility. Collaborations can take the form of sponsored content, guest posts, or joint events.

Conclusion

Building a successful digital antique shop requires a seamless combination of a well-curated collection, an engaging digital storefront, and effective marketing strategies. By focusing on creating an appealing and user-friendly website and leveraging a variety of marketing channels, you can attract and retain customers, establish your brand within your niche, and grow your business.

In the coming chapters, we will explore the importance of customer service and building long-lasting relationships with your customers, as well as strategies for continually evolving and adapting your digital antique shop to stay ahead of the competition in the ever-changing digital landscape.

By mastering the art of digital storefront design, marketing, and customer engagement, you will be well on your way to creating a thriving digital antique shop that not only captivates the hearts and minds of antique enthusiasts around the world but also stands the test of time in the dynamic and competitive world of e-commerce.

Chapter 6: Exceptional Customer Service and Building Long-Lasting Relationships

In the digital world, exceptional customer service is a crucial aspect of establishing and maintaining a successful antique shop. By creating memorable experiences and building strong relationships with your customers, you can cultivate loyalty, encourage repeat business, and generate word-of-mouth referrals. In this chapter, we will discuss strategies for providing outstanding customer service and fostering long-lasting connections with your clientele.

Creating Memorable Customer Experiences

To create memorable and satisfying customer experiences, consider the following strategies:

- Offer Personalized Recommendations: Use your knowledge and expertise in your niche to provide personalized recommendations based on each customer's interests, preferences, and needs. By taking the time to understand your customers, you can guide them towards items that resonate with them on a deeper level.
- Be Responsive and Accessible: Respond promptly and professionally to customer inquiries, whether via email, social media, or live chat. Ensure that your contact information is clearly displayed on your website and provide multiple channels for customers to reach you.
- Share Your Passion and Expertise: Share your passion for antiques and your unique insights with your customers, whether through engaging product descriptions, informative blog posts, or personalized interactions. This will help you establish credibility and build trust with your customers.
- Provide Clear and Transparent Policies: Establish and communicate clear policies regarding shipping, returns, and refunds. Make sure these policies are easily accessible on your website and provide detailed instructions on how customers can initiate a return or exchange.
- Go the Extra Mile: Surprise and delight your customers by going beyond their expectations. This could include offering complimentary gift wrapping, including a handwritten thank-you note with each order, or providing unexpected upgrades or discounts.

Building Long-Lasting Relationships

Fostering strong relationships with your customers can lead to increased customer loyalty, repeat business, and referrals. Consider the following tactics to build long-lasting connections with your clientele:

- Establish a Loyalty Program: Create a loyalty program that rewards customers for repeat business. Offer exclusive discounts, first access to new arrivals, or other rewards to increase customer loyalty.
- Engage with Your Customers on Social Media: Actively engage with your customers on social media platforms by responding to comments, sharing user-generated content, and creating opportunities for interaction, such as polls, giveaways, or live events.
- Send Personalized Follow-Up Communications: Reach out to your customers after a purchase to express your gratitude, ask for feedback, or help. This distinctive touch can go a long way in establishing rapport and building trust.
- Host Online Events and Workshops: Organize virtual events or workshops related to your niche, such as webinars on antique restoration, live auctions, or virtual tours of your shop. These events can help you connect with your customers, display your expertise, and create a sense of community around your brand.
- Solicit Feedback and Act on It: Encourage customers to provide feedback and reviews and be responsive to their suggestions and concerns. Show your customers that you value their opinions and are committed to continuously improving their shopping experience.

Conclusion

Exceptional customer service and strong relationships with your customers are essential components of a thriving digital antique shop. By focusing on creating memorable experiences and fostering genuine connections with your clientele, you can cultivate a loyal customer base that will support your business for years to come.

In the last chapter, we will discuss strategies for continually evolving and adapting your digital antique shop to stay ahead of the competition, seize new opportunities, and thrive in the dynamic world of e-commerce. By embracing change and innovation, you can ensure that your digital antique shop remains relevant, captivating, and successful in the ever-evolving digital landscape.

Chapter 7: Adapting and Evolving in the Digital World

Success in the digital antique business requires not only a well-curated collection, an engaging digital storefront, and exceptional customer service, but also the ability to adapt and evolve in the rapidly changing digital landscape. In this last chapter, we will explore strategies for staying ahead of the curve, embracing innovation, and ensuring your digital antique shop remains relevant and successful for years to come.

Staying Informed and Embracing Innovation

To stay ahead of the competition and seize new opportunities, it is essential to stay informed and embrace innovation. Consider the following strategies:

- Monitor Trends and Market Developments: Regularly research and analyze trends within the antique market and the broader e-commerce industry. This will help you identify new opportunities, adapt your marketing strategies, and make informed decisions about your inventory and business operations.
- Invest in Technology: Explore and adopt recent technologies and tools that can streamline your business processes, enhance your digital storefront, or improve your marketing efforts. This could include implementing artificial intelligence (AI) for personalized recommendations, adopting augmented reality (AR) to create immersive online shopping experiences, or using chatbots to assist with customer inquiries.
- Diversify Your Marketing Channels: Continually evaluate and experiment with current marketing channels and platforms to expand your reach and connect with new audiences. This could include trying new advertising formats, exploring emerging social media platforms, or leveraging influencer partnerships.
- Participate in Industry Events and Networking: Attend conferences, workshops, and networking events within the antique and e-commerce communities to stay informed about new developments, learn from industry experts, and build relationships with other professionals.
- Cultivate a Culture of Continuous Learning: Encourage a culture of continuous learning within your team by providing opportunities for professional development, sharing industry news and insights, and fostering a collaborative and open-minded work environment.

Embracing change and innovation is crucial for ensuring your digital antique shop remains relevant and successful. Consider the following strategies for adapting and evolving your business:

- Regularly Evaluate and Update Your Inventory: Continually assess your inventory to ensure it reflects current trends, customer preferences, and your unique brand identity. Be prepared to pivot your collection and sourcing strategies as needed to stay ahead of the competition.
- Optimize Your Digital Storefront: Regularly review and update your website to ensure it remains visually appealing, user-friendly, and optimized for search engines. Continuously refine your product descriptions, images, and overall site design to improve the customer experience.
- Experiment with New Business Models: Explore new business models or revenue streams that can complement your existing digital antique shop, such as offering antique appraisal services, organizing virtual events, or launching a subscription box service.
- Seek Feedback and Act on It: Continuously seek feedback from your customers, peers, and industry experts to identify areas for improvement and growth. Be open to constructive criticism and be prepared to make necessary changes to your business operations, marketing strategies, or inventory.
- Embrace Collaboration and Partnerships: Cultivate relationships within the antique and e-commerce communities, and seek out opportunities for collaboration, partnerships, or mentorship. By working together and learning from others, you can unlock new opportunities and drive innovation within your digital antique shop.

Conclusion

The journey to creating a successful digital antique shop is one of continuous learning, adaptation, and evolution. By staying informed, embracing innovation, and fostering a culture of continuous improvement, you can ensure that your digital antique shop remains relevant, captivating, and successful in the ever-changing world of e-commerce.

As you embark on your journey to becoming a digital antique shop owner, remember that success lies in your passion, determination, and commitment to excellence with a well-curated collection.

Chapter 8: Planning for Long-Term Success and Growth

As you lay the foundation for your digital antique shop, it is essential to look beyond the initial setup and plan for long-term success and growth. In this chapter, we will discuss strategies for setting goals, tracking progress, and continuously evolving your business to ensure lasting success and sustainability.

Setting Goals and Tracking Progress

Establishing clear objectives and monitoring your progress will help you make informed decisions, allocate resources effectively, and maintain focus on your long-term vision. Consider the following strategies for setting goals and tracking progress:

- Develop a Business Plan: Create a comprehensive business plan that outlines your mission, vision, target market, goals, and strategies for achieving success. This document will serve as a roadmap for your business, guiding you through the various stages of growth and helping you stay on track.
- Set SMART Goals: Establish Specific, Measurable, Achievable, Relevant, and Time-bound (SMART) goals for your digital antique shop. These goals should be aligned with your overall business plan and cover various aspects of your business, including sales, marketing, customer service, and inventory management.
- Monitor Key Performance Indicators (KPIs): Identify and track relevant KPIs to evaluate your progress towards your goals. KPIs can include metrics such as website traffic, conversion rates, average order value, customer lifetime value, and social media engagement.
- Conduct Regular Performance Reviews: Regularly review your progress against your goals and KPIs, and adjust your strategies as needed to stay on track. Be prepared to pivot and adapt to changes in the market, customer preferences, or competitive landscape.
- Celebrate Milestones and Learn from Failures: Recognize and celebrate your achievements, however small, as they can serve as motivation and inspiration for your team. Equally important, embrace failures as learning opportunities and use them to refine your strategies and grow your business.

Planning for Long-Term Growth and Sustainability

To ensure the long-term success and sustainability of your digital antique shop, consider the following strategies:

- Cultivate a Loyal Customer Base: Focus on building strong relationships with your customers and providing exceptional customer experiences to encourage repeat business and word-of-mouth referrals.
- Diversify Your Revenue Streams: Explore opportunities to expand your product offerings or introduce complementary services, such as antique restoration, appraisals, or consulting, to diversify your revenue streams and mitigate risk.
- Continuously Improve Your Online Presence: Regularly update and optimize your website, social media channels, and marketing strategies to stay current with industry trends, best practices, and customer preferences.
- Invest in Your Team: Attract, retain, and develop a talented team that shares your passion for antiques and is committed to the success of your digital antique shop. Provide ongoing training and professional development opportunities to ensure your team stays up to date with industry trends and best practices.
- Plan for Succession: Develop a succession plan that outlines how your digital antique shop will be managed and operated in the event of your retirement, disability, or death. This plan should include details on leadership transition, financial arrangements, and operational processes to ensure the long-term sustainability of your business.

Conclusion

Building a successful digital antique shop requires not only passion and determination but also a commitment to long-term planning and growth. By setting clear goals, tracking progress, and continuously evolving your business, you can create a thriving and sustainable digital antique shop that will stand the test of time.

As you embark on your journey as a digital antique shop owner, remember that success is not a destination but a journey. With a well-curated collection, an engaging digital storefront, exceptional customer service, and a focus on long-term growth and sustainability, you can create a digital antique shop that captivates the hearts and minds of antique enthusiasts around the world, while standing the test of time in the dynamic and competitive world of e-commerce.

As you progress on this exciting journey, never lose sight of your passion for antiques and the unique stories they hold. Stay true to your vision, embrace innovation, and cultivate a community of loyal customers and supporters. With dedication, resilience, and adaptability, you can create a digital antique shop that not only flourishes in the present but also thrives well into the future.

In conclusion, the blueprint for becoming a successful antique shop owner in the digital world consists of a well-rounded strategy that encompasses sourcing, marketing, customer service, innovation, and long-term planning. By following the guidance provided in this book and staying true to your passion for antiques, you will be well-equipped to navigate the ever-changing digital landscape and build a lasting and successful business.

Now, it is time to take the first step on your journey and begin creating the digital antique shop of your dreams. Remember that success is a journey, not a destination. Embrace the challenges and opportunities that lie ahead, and never lose sight of your passion for antiques and the unique stories they hold. Best of luck with your exciting new venture!

Chapter 9: Embracing the Digital Antique Shop Community

In the digital world, building a sense of community around your antique shop is crucial for creating a loyal customer base, fostering collaboration, and driving long-term success. In this chapter, we will discuss strategies for engaging with the digital antique community, collaborating with fellow enthusiasts, and positioning your business as a valuable member of the online antique world.

Connecting with the Digital Antique Community

By actively participating in the digital antique community, you can build relationships, learn from others, and create a supportive network of like-minded individuals. Consider the following strategies for connecting with the online antique community:

- Join Online Forums and Groups: Seek out and engage in online forums and groups dedicated to antiques and collectibles. Share your knowledge, ask questions, and participate in discussions to build connections with fellow enthusiasts and experts.
- Attend Virtual Events and Conferences: Attend online conferences, webinars, and other virtual events focused on antiques and e-commerce. These events provide opportunities for networking, learning, and staying current with industry trends.
- Follow Industry Influencers and Experts: Follow and engage with antique influencers, experts, and fellow shop owners on social media platforms, such as Instagram, Facebook, and Twitter. Share their content, ask questions, and participate in discussions to build relationships and increase your visibility within the community.

- Collaborate on Content Creation: Partner with other antique shop owners, collectors, or experts to create content, such as blog posts, videos, or podcasts. Collaborating on content not only helps you learn from others but also exposes your brand to new audiences.
- Share Your Story and Passion: Use your digital platform to share your passion for antiques, your personal journey, and the unique story behind your shop. By being open and authentic, you can create a sense of connection with your audience and foster a sense of community around your brand.

Fostering Collaboration and Support

Collaboration and support within the digital antique community can lead to new opportunities, increased knowledge, and a more resilient and successful business. Consider the following strategies for fostering collaboration and support:

- Establish Partnerships and Alliances: Form strategic partnerships with other antique shop owners, suppliers, or industry professionals. These partnerships can lead to joint marketing efforts, shared resources, or other collaborative opportunities that benefit both parties.
- Offer Support and Mentorship: Share your expertise and experience with fellow antique shop owners or enthusiasts who may be just starting their journey. By offering support and mentorship, you can build strong relationships and establish yourself as a respected member of the community.
- Participate in Community Projects: Engage in community-driven projects, such as virtual antique fairs, online auctions, or charity events. These projects not only provide opportunities for collaboration but also

contribute to the overall growth and success of the digital antique community.

- Create a Shared Learning Environment: Organize virtual workshops, webinars, or discussion groups that focus on topics related to antiques, e-commerce, or business management. By providing a platform for shared learning and growth, you can foster a sense of community and collaboration among fellow enthusiasts and professionals.
- Celebrate the Success of Others: Acknowledge and celebrate the achievements of others within the digital antique community. Share their success stories on your social media channels, congratulate them in online forums or groups, and express your support and encouragement.

Conclusion

By embracing the digital antique shop community, you can create a dedicated support network, learn from fellow enthusiasts and experts, and contribute to the overall growth and success of the online antique world. By actively participating in the community, collaborating with others, and fostering a sense of connection and support, you can position your digital antique shop as a valuable and respected member of the online antique community.

As you continue your journey as a digital antique shop owner, remember that building a successful business is not just about the products you sell or the strategies you employ but also about the connections you make and the community you become a part of. By engaging with the digital antique community, you can create a thriving and supportive network that not only benefits your business but also contributes to the overall growth and success of the antique world.

As you forge connections, share knowledge, and collaborate with fellow antique enthusiasts and professionals, you will discover that the digital antique shop community is a vibrant and inspiring place to be. Embrace the opportunity to learn from others, share your passion, and contribute to the success of this dynamic and ever-evolving community.

With an intense sense of community, innovative strategies, and a commitment to continuous improvement, your digital antique shop will not only succeed in the competitive e-commerce landscape but also become a cherished destination for antique lovers across the globe. So, dive into the digital antique community, forge lasting connections, and continue to grow and evolve as a digital antique shop owner. The future is bright, and the possibilities are endless.

Chapter 10: Measuring and Celebrating Success in the Digital Antique World

As your digital antique shop grows and evolves, it is essential to take the time to measure your achievements and celebrate your successes. In this last chapter, we will discuss strategies for evaluating your accomplishments, recognizing the demanding work of your team, and celebrating the milestones that define your journey as a digital antique shop owner.

Evaluating Your Accomplishments

Measuring success goes beyond just financial gains; it also encompasses personal growth, the impact on your community, and the satisfaction of your customers. Consider the following strategies for evaluating your accomplishments:

- Reflect on Your Goals: Revisit your business plan and SMART goals regularly to assess your progress and determine whether you are on track to achieve your objectives. This will help you identify areas of success, as well as opportunities for improvement.

- Analyze Your KPIs: Review your Key Performance Indicators (KPIs) to measure the performance of your digital antique shop across various aspects, such as sales, marketing, customer service, and inventory management. This will provide valuable insights into the overall health and growth of your business.
- Gather Customer Feedback: Collect and analyze customer feedback to gauge their satisfaction and identify areas where you are exceeding expectations or falling short. This feedback can also help you uncover new opportunities for growth or improvement.
- Assess Your Impact on the Community: Consider the impact your digital antique shop has on the broader antique community and your local community. This could include your contributions to industry events, collaborations with fellow shop owners, or support for local causes and charities.
- Reflect on Personal Growth: Take the time to evaluate your personal growth and development as a digital antique shop owner. Consider the skills you have acquired, the knowledge you have gained, and the challenges you have overcome throughout your journey.

Recognizing and Celebrating Success

Celebrating success is an essential part of your journey as a digital antique shop owner. It not only boosts morale and motivation but also helps create a culture of appreciation and continuous improvement. Consider the following strategies for recognizing and celebrating success:

- Acknowledge Individual Achievements: Recognize the hard work and accomplishments of your team members, both publicly and privately. This could include praising their efforts in team meetings, highlighting their achievements on social media, or providing personalized feedback and words of encouragement.

- Celebrate Milestones: Commemorate significant milestones, such as reaching a specific number of sales, expanding your inventory, or celebrating your shop's anniversary. These celebrations can be as simple as a team lunch, a social media post, or a small gift for your employees.
- Share Success Stories: Share your success stories with your customers and the broader digital antique community. This could include highlighting positive customer reviews, highlighting unique finds, or sharing stories of collaboration and community involvement.
- Reflect on Lessons Learned: Embrace both successes and failures as opportunities for growth and improvement. Reflect on the lessons learned from your experiences and use them to refine your strategies and drive continuous improvement.
- Encourage a Culture of Appreciation: Foster a work environment where appreciation, recognition, and celebration are integral parts of your team's culture. This will help create a positive atmosphere and motivate your team to continually strive for success.

Conclusion

As you conclude your journey through this blueprint for becoming a successful digital antique shop owner, remember that success is a continuous journey marked by achievements, challenges, and growth. By regularly evaluating your accomplishments, recognizing the demanding work of your team, and celebrating your successes, you can create a thriving, resilient, and sustainable digital antique business.

As you forge ahead in the world of digital antiques, hold onto your passion for the unique stories and history that each piece holds. Embrace the challenges, celebrate the victories, and continue to grow and evolve as a digital antique shop owner. Your passion, dedication, and commitment to excellence will not only drive the success of your business but also inspire others within the antique community.

Remember that the digital antique world is ever-changing, and staying adaptable, innovative, and connected to your community is crucial to your long-term success. As you continue to learn, grow, and thrive, your digital antique shop will become a cherished destination for antique enthusiasts across the globe.

In conclusion, the journey of becoming a successful digital antique shop owner is a rewarding and fulfilling adventure. By following the strategies outlined in this book and staying true to your passion for antiques, you will be well-equipped to navigate the dynamic world of e-commerce and create a lasting, successful business. As you move forward, cherish the connections you forge, the milestones you reach, and the unique stories you uncover through your love for antiques.

Chapter 11: Embracing Sustainability and Social Responsibility in the Digital Antique World

In the ever-evolving world of e-commerce and antiques, embracing sustainability and social responsibility is not only a moral obligation but also a competitive advantage. In this chapter, we will discuss strategies for incorporating sustainable practices and socially responsible values into your digital antique shop, helping you create a business that is not only successful but also a force for good.

Sustainable Practices for Your Digital Antique Shop

Incorporating sustainable practices into your digital antique shop can help reduce your environmental footprint, support ethical practices, and appeal to eco-conscious customers. Consider the following strategies for promoting sustainability:

- Source Responsibly: When acquiring antiques, ensure they come from reputable and ethical sources. Avoid items obtained through illegal or harmful means, such as looting, theft, or exploitation.
- Reuse and Repurpose: Embrace the ethos of reusing and repurposing by offering antiques and vintage items that give new life to old treasures. This helps reduce waste and promotes a circular economy.
- Adopt Eco-friendly Packaging: Use recyclable, biodegradable, or reusable packaging materials when shipping your antiques. This reduces waste and minimizes your shop's environmental impact.
- Promote Energy Efficiency: Implement energy-efficient practices within your workspace, such as using LED lighting, conserving water, and utilizing energy-saving appliances.
- Encourage Green Transportation: When possible, use environmentally friendly shipping options or work with logistics providers that prioritize sustainable practices.

Social Responsibility in Your Digital Antique Shop

Being a socially responsible business means actively contributing to the well-being of society and supporting ethical practices. Consider the following strategies for promoting social responsibility:

- Support Local Artisans and Craftspeople: Whenever possible, source antiques and vintage items from local artisans and craftspeople. This supports your local economy and preserves cultural heritage.
- Prioritize Fair Trade and Ethical Supply Chains: Work with suppliers that prioritize fair trade, fair labor practices, and

ethical sourcing. This ensures that your business supports ethical practices and contributes positively to the global community.

- Give Back to Your Community: Engage in philanthropic efforts or support local charities and causes that align with your values. This can include donating a portion of your profits, volunteering, or sponsoring events and initiatives.
- Advocate for Diversity and Inclusion: Foster a diverse and inclusive workplace by hiring employees from various backgrounds and promoting an inclusive culture. In addition, support organizations and initiatives that promote diversity and inclusion within the antique community and beyond.
- Educate and Inspire: Use your digital platform to educate your customers and followers about sustainability, social responsibility, and the importance of preserving cultural heritage. This can help inspire others to make more sustainable and socially responsible choices in their own lives.

By embracing sustainability and social responsibility, you can create a digital antique shop that not only thrives in the competitive e-commerce landscape but also positively impacts the world. Incorporating sustainable practices and socially responsible values into your business can help you attract eco-conscious customers, foster a positive brand image, and contribute to the well-being of society and the environment.

As you continue your journey as a digital antique shop owner, remember that your success is not just defined by your financial achievements, but also by the positive impact you make on the world around you. By staying true to your passion for antiques and prioritizing sustainability and social responsibility, you can build a lasting, successful business that stands the test of time and serves as a force for good in the digital antique world.

Chapter 11: Building a Legacy as a Digital Antique Shop Owner

As you embark on your journey as a digital antique shop owner, it is essential to think beyond short-term success and consider the long-term legacy you wish to leave behind. In this chapter, we will discuss strategies for creating a lasting impact, nurturing the next generation of antique enthusiasts, and building a business that stands the test of time.

Creating a Lasting Impact

To create a lasting impact with your digital antique shop, focus on delivering exceptional value to your customers, preserving cultural heritage, and fostering a sense of community. Consider the following strategies:

- Offer Unmatched Customer Experiences: Strive to create memorable and personalized experiences for your customers by providing exceptional service, expert knowledge, and unique products.
- Preserve and Share Cultural Heritage: Use your digital platform to educate and inspire others about the historical and cultural significance of the antiques you offer. This helps promote the appreciation and preservation of our shared heritage.
- Build a Strong and Loyal Community: Cultivate a dedicated community of antique enthusiasts by engaging with them through social media, online forums, and virtual events. By fostering a sense of connection, you create a lasting impact on your customers and the broader antique community.
- Continuously Evolve and Adapt: Stay ahead of industry trends and embrace recent technologies to ensure your digital antique shop remains relevant and successful in the ever-changing e-commerce landscape.

Nurturing the Next Generation of Antique Enthusiasts

To ensure the continued appreciation and preservation of antiques, it is essential to inspire and nurture the next generation of antique enthusiasts. Consider the following strategies:

- Create Educational Content: Develop engaging and informative content, such as blog posts, videos, or webinars, to educate younger audiences about the world of antiques and the importance of preserving cultural heritage.
- Collaborate with Schools and Educational Institutions: Partner with schools and educational institutions to offer workshops, lectures, or tours that introduce students to the

world of antiques and the importance of cultural preservation.

- Offer Internships and Mentorships: Provide opportunities for young people to gain hands-on experience in the antique industry through internships or mentorship programs. This not only helps them develop valuable skills but also fosters their passion for antiques.
- Support Youth-Focused Initiatives: Participate in or sponsor initiatives that promote the appreciation of antiques and cultural heritage among younger generations, such as youth-focused antique fairs, workshops, or competitions.

Building a Business That Stands the Test of Time

To build a digital antique shop that endures, focus on cultivating a strong brand identity, implementing sound business practices, and planning for the future. Consider the following strategies:

- Develop a Unique and Recognizable Brand: Establish a strong brand identity that reflects your passion for antiques and resonates with your target audience. This helps set you apart from competitors and creates an impression.
- Implement Strong Business Practices: Adopt sound business practices, such as effective inventory management, financial planning, and marketing strategies, to ensure the long-term success and stability of your digital antique shop.
- Plan for Succession: Develop a succession plan to ensure the continuity and preservation of your digital antique shop. This may involve training family members, identifying potential successors, or establishing partnerships with other antique professionals.
- Stay Committed to Your Vision: Stay true to your passion for antiques and your commitment to preserving cultural heritage. By remaining focused on your core values and vision, you can build a business that stands the test of time.

Conclusion

Building a legacy as a digital antique shop owner involves creating a lasting impact on your customers and the broader antique community, nurturing the next generation of antique enthusiasts, and establishing a business that endures. By following the strategies outlined in this chapter, you can create a digital antique shop that not only achieves financial success but also contributes to the preservation of cultural heritage and the continued appreciation of antiques for generations to come.

As you move forward on your journey as a digital antique shop owner, remember that your legacy is shaped by the connections you forge, the knowledge you share, and the passion you bring to the world of antiques. Embrace the opportunity to inspire others, contribute to the preservation of history, and create a lasting impact in the digital antique world.

In conclusion, building a legacy as a digital antique shop owner is a rewarding and fulfilling endeavor that requires dedication, passion, and a commitment to the long-term success and impact of your business. By embracing the strategies outlined in this book and staying true to your passion for antiques, you can create a lasting, successful business that enriches the lives of antique enthusiasts, preserves our shared cultural heritage, and inspires future generations to appreciate the unique stories and history that each antique piece holds.

Chapter 12: Expanding Your Digital Antique Empire

In this last chapter, we will explore strategies for taking your digital antique shop to the next level by expanding your reach, diversifying your offerings, and leveraging collaborations and partnerships. By following these strategies, you can transform your digital antique shop into a thriving digital antique empire.

Scaling Your Digital Antique Shop

To expand your digital antique shop, consider the following strategies for scaling your business:

- Expand Your Product Offerings: Broaden your inventory by introducing new categories of antiques or vintage items. This can help attract a wider audience and increase your overall revenue.
- Tap into New Markets: Research and identify new markets where there is a demand for antiques and vintage items. This could include targeting specific regions, countries, or demographic groups.
- Optimize Your Online Presence: Improve your website's user experience, search engine optimization (SEO), and mobile responsiveness to attract more visitors and increase your online visibility.
- Enhance Your Marketing Efforts: Invest in strategic marketing initiatives, such as social media advertising, email campaigns, and content marketing, to reach new customers and strengthen your brand presence.

Diversifying Your Antique Business

Diversification can help mitigate risks, tap into new revenue streams, and increase the resilience of your digital antique empire. Consider the following strategies for diversifying your business:

- Offer Appraisal Services: Provide antique appraisal services to help customers determine the value of their items. This can help position you as an authority in the industry and generate additional income.
- Host Virtual Events and Workshops: Organize virtual events, such as webinars, workshops, or live auctions, to engage with your customers, share your expertise, and create additional revenue streams.

- Launch a Private Label or Custom Collection: Create a private label or custom collection of antique-inspired items, such as furniture, home décor, or jewelry, to diversify your product offerings and appeal to a wider audience.
- Offer Restoration and Conservation Services: Partner with skilled artisans to provide restoration and conservation services for antiques and vintage items, adding value to your customers' cherished possessions.

Leveraging Collaborations and Partnerships

Collaborations and partnerships can help expand your reach, increase your credibility, and generate new business opportunities. Consider the following strategies for leveraging collaborations and partnerships:

- Collaborate with Influencers and Experts: Partner with antique influencers, historians, or experts to co-create content, promote your digital antique shop, or host virtual events.
- Join Forces with Fellow Antique Shop Owners: Form alliances with other digital antique shop owners to cross-promote your businesses, share industry insights, or collaborate on special projects.
- Partner with Nonprofit Organizations or Cultural Institutions: Work with museums, historical societies, or nonprofit organizations to promote the preservation of cultural heritage and support initiatives that align with your business values.
- Establish Strategic Business Partnerships: Partner with complementary businesses, such as interior designers, event planners, or vintage clothing retailers, to cross-promote your offerings and tap into new customer segments.

Expanding your digital antique empire requires strategic planning, diversification, and collaboration. By implementing the strategies outlined in this chapter, you can scale your business, reach new markets, and create a thriving digital antique empire that stands the test of time.

As you continue your journey in the world of digital antiques, remember that the key to long-term success is constant adaptation, innovation, and a commitment to delivering exceptional value to your customers. By staying true to your passion for antiques and embracing the opportunities that come with growth and expansion, you can create a digital antique empire that not only achieves financial success but also contributes to the preservation and appreciation of our shared cultural heritage.

May your digital antique empire continue to grow and flourish and may your passion for antiques inspire others to explore and appreciate the rich history and unique stories that each piece holds. As you forge ahead, always remember that the legacy you create as a digital antique shop owner is not only about the success of your business but also about the impact you have on the lives of your customers, the antique community, and the preservation of cultural heritage.

By staying true to your values, nurturing relationships, and continuously evolving in the ever-changing digital landscape, you can create a lasting, successful digital antique empire that enriches the lives of countless antique enthusiasts and inspires future generations to cherish the beauty and history of the antiques they encounter.

Chapter 13: Celebrating Milestones and Navigating Challenges in the Digital Antique World

In this chapter, we will explore the importance of celebrating milestones and navigating the inevitable challenges that arise in the ever-evolving digital antique world. By acknowledging your accomplishments and learning from adversity, you can continue to grow and thrive as a digital antique shop owner.

Celebrating Milestones

Acknowledging and celebrating milestones is essential for maintaining motivation, fostering a sense of accomplishment, and building momentum for your digital antique shop. Consider the following strategies for celebrating milestones:

- Set Specific, Measurable Goals: Establish clear, achievable goals for your digital antique shop, such as revenue targets, website traffic, or social media followers. These milestones will help you track your progress and measure your success.
- Share Your Achievements: Share your accomplishments with your customers, followers, and the antique community by posting updates on social media, your website, or through email newsletters. This not only fosters a sense of community but also helps build your brand's reputation.
- Treat Yourself: Reward yourself and your team for reaching milestones, whether it's a small celebration, a token of appreciation, or a well-deserved break. This helps maintain motivation and foster a positive work environment.
- Reflect and Learn: Regularly review your progress, identify areas for improvement, and celebrate your achievements. This reflection process helps you learn from both your successes and setbacks, ensuring continuous growth and improvement.

Navigating Challenges in the Digital Antique World

Running a digital antique shop comes with its share of challenges, from changing market trends to unforeseen obstacles. By developing resilience and problem-solving skills, you can navigate these challenges with confidence. Consider the following strategies for overcoming adversity:

- Embrace Change: Stay adaptable and open to change, as the digital antique world is constantly evolving. This may involve updating your inventory, adopting new technologies, or adjusting your marketing strategies.
- Develop a Strong Support Network: Build a network of peers, mentors, and industry experts who can provide guidance, support, and encouragement during challenging times.
- Cultivate a Growth Mindset: View challenges as opportunities for growth and learning, rather than setbacks. This mindset can help you approach difficulties with a positive attitude and a determination to succeed.
- Seek Out Resources: Leverage educational resources, such as online courses, webinars, or industry workshops, to develop new skills and enhance your problem-solving abilities.
- Stay Focused on Your Vision: Remember your passion for antiques and your commitment to preserving cultural heritage. By staying true to your vision and values, you can maintain motivation and resilience during challenging times.

As a digital antique shop owner, celebrating milestones and navigating challenges are essential aspects of your journey to success. By acknowledging your accomplishments, fostering resilience, and learning from adversity, you can continue to grow and thrive in the dynamic world of digital antiques.

In this ever-evolving industry, stay true to your passion, embrace change, and foster a spirit of continuous learning and improvement. By doing so, you can overcome challenges, celebrate your successes, and build a lasting, successful digital antique shop that stands the test of time.

As you continue your journey in the digital antique world, remember that your passion, dedication, and resilience are the keys to unlocking your full potential as a digital antique shop owner. Embrace the milestones and challenges that come your way and let them shape your path to success in the fascinating world of antiques and e-commerce.

Chapter 14: Leaving a Positive Impact on the Digital Antique Community

In this chapter, we will explore the ways in which you, as a digital antique shop owner, can leave a positive impact on the digital antique community. By fostering a sense of unity, supporting fellow antique professionals, and contributing to the preservation of cultural heritage, you can create a legacy that benefits not only your business but also the entire digital antique community.

Creating a Sense of Unity

Cultivating a sense of unity among antique enthusiasts is crucial for maintaining the vibrancy and appeal of the digital antique community. Consider the following strategies for fostering a sense of unity:

- Build an Engaging Online Community: Use social media, online forums, and virtual events to create a welcoming space for antique enthusiasts to connect, share their passion, and exchange knowledge.
- Encourage Collaboration and Cooperation: Facilitate collaborative projects, such as virtual antique fairs, joint marketing campaigns, or knowledge-sharing events, that bring together antique professionals and enthusiasts.
- Share Your Expertise: Provide valuable insights, tips, and resources to help others in the digital antique community learn and grow. This not only positions you as an industry authority but also contributes to the overall success of the community.

Supporting Fellow Antique Professionals

Supporting your fellow antique professionals is essential for maintaining a thriving digital antique community. Consider the following strategies for extending your support:

- Promote and Celebrate the Success of Others: Share and celebrate the achievements of fellow antique professionals on your social media platforms or through collaborative events. This fosters a supportive environment and helps build strong relationships within the community.

- Offer Mentorship and Guidance: Share your expertise and knowledge with up-and-coming antique professionals, helping them navigate the challenges of the digital antique world and ensuring the continued growth and success of the community.
- Engage in Knowledge Sharing: Participate in industry events, conferences, or webinars to exchange ideas and best practices with your peers. This not only keeps you informed but also helps strengthen the digital antique community.

Contributing to Cultural Heritage Preservation

As a digital antique shop owner, you have a unique opportunity to contribute to the preservation of cultural heritage. Consider the following strategies for making a positive impact:

- Educate the Public: Use your digital platform to raise awareness about the historical and cultural significance of antiques and the importance of preserving them for future generations.
- Support Preservation Initiatives: Partner with or contribute to nonprofit organizations, museums, or historical societies that work to preserve cultural heritage. This not only supports their efforts but also aligns your business with a noble cause.
- Advocate for Responsible Antique Ownership: Promote responsible antique ownership by educating customers on proper care, restoration, and conservation techniques, ensuring the continued preservation of these valuable artifacts.

Conclusion

Leaving a positive impact on the digital antique community is a crucial aspect of your journey as a digital antique shop owner. By fostering a sense of unity, supporting fellow antique professionals, and contributing to the preservation of cultural heritage, you can create a legacy that benefits the entire digital antique community.

As you continue to build your digital antique shop, remember that your success is intertwined with the success of the broader digital antique community. Embrace the opportunity to make a positive impact and let your passion for antiques inspire others to join this vibrant and diverse community.

Together, we can ensure that the digital antique world remains a thriving, dynamic space where the beauty, history, and cultural significance of antiques are celebrated and preserved for generations to come.

www.ingramcontent.com/pod-product-compliance
Lightning Source LLC
Chambersburg PA
CBHW071111220526
45467CB00004B/1813